Essential Preparation for

UMAT

UNDERGRADUATE MEDICINE & HEALTH SCIENCES ADMISSION TEST

Series Three

BOOK 1
LOGICAL REASONING
& PROBLEM SOLVING

Mohan Dhall

Five Senses Education Pty Ltd
2/195 Prospect Highway
Seven Hills 2147
New South Wales
Australia

Dhall, Mohan
Series 3, Book 1 - Logical Reasoning & Problem Solving

ISBN 978-1-76032-006-5

CONTENTS

Introduction to UMAT and the Trial Test Papers

Students can gain access into medical training in Australia in one of three ways:

- Through post-graduate entry following the completion of an undergraduate degree. This degree should be in science or science related subjects and the student will need to achieve a high Grade Point Average (GPA).

- Through direct entry based on Year 12 results

- Through performance on the UMAT test and interview (done by each participating university, depending on UMAT results)

The purpose of the UMAT entry test is to assist in the selection of candidates who display the requisite thinking skills and abilities for successful medical training. The test is a 3-hour test completed under exam conditions. There are 134 questions based around three different types of thinking and reasoning:

1. Logical reasoning and problem-solving (48 questions)
2. Understanding people skills (44 questions)
3. Non-verbal reasoning (42 questions)

The follow-up interview performed by participating universities can be quite demanding and can take up to an hour, before a panel of up to three interviewers. Thus preparation and the development of appropriate interview skills and techniques should be practiced, in addition to undertaking test-training.

UMAT Logical Reasoning and Problem-Solving Questions

There are 48 practice questions here

Students should aim to take about 70 minutes to complete them. There are practice answer sheets at the end of this book. Try not to mark the pages of the book, as you will be able to repeat the questions and test yourself several times.

Instructions to Candidates

The questions here help students to develop and hone their logical thinking skills, reasoning abilities, capacity to deduce from known facts, make conclusions and test assumptions against facts.

The questions are presented in different forms: graphical, textual, tabular and visual. Students should aim to familiarise themselves with each form of stimulus.

The questions are based on ideas about problem solving and critical thinking as key processes in making rational decisions. Elements of these reasoning processes are considered, such as the ability to identify the problem and relevant information; to comprehend, analyse, select, transform, synthesise and evaluate information; to generate and test hypotheses and solutions; and to draw conclusions. The questions have a common general reasoning focus and employ both text-based and text-free reasoning and both inductive and deductive reasoning. Questions are based on information that is generally non-medical and non-technical. No curriculum-specific knowledge is required (beyond basic literacy and numeracy) to understand the materials and to arrive at the correct answers. However, non-specialist scientific contexts may be used and the application of common-sense, everyday scientific methodology is expected.

Logical Reasoning & Problem Solving Questions

Question 1

Complete the pattern

1, 2, 2, 4, 2, 4

A) 2, 2, 6, 2, 8
B) 2, 4, 6, 2, 6
C) 2, 1, 2, 4, 8
D) 4, 2, 4, 2, 6

Question 2

What is the next number in this pattern?

12, 4, 3, 1.33, 2.25

A) 3.50
B) 0.33
C) 0.59
D) 4.50

Questions 3 - 5

Types of bone marrow transplant include:

1. Autologous BMT – Cells come from the patient's own bone marrow
2. Allogeneic BMT – The cells come from a matched related or unrelated donor
3. Syngeneic BMT – The cells are derived from an identical twin.

Autologous stem cell transplant

The patient's own bone marrow cells are taken prior to the anti-cancer procedure. These stem cells are removed, or harvested, from either bone marrow or blood and then frozen. After this, a high dose of chemotherapy or radiation therapy is given. Once the bone marrow is suppressed the frozen cells are thawed and replaced back within the body. The advantage is that the patient gets his or her own blood cells and thus there is a decreased risk of the body's immune system not recognising the cells and rejecting them or mounting an attack on them. This is called graft rejection and rejection makes allogenic transplants (discussed below) difficult. The disadvantage of the process is the risk of the originally taken stem cells carrying cancer cells that are reintroduced into the body. This may bring the cancer back.

What is autologous stem cell transplant used for?

This kind of transplant is mainly used to treat some leukemias and lymphomas, and multiple myeloma. It is sometimes used for other cancers, especially in children. In a tandem transplant, a patient gets 2 courses of high-dose chemo, each followed by a transplant of their own stem cells. All of the stem cells needed are collected before the first high-dose chemo treatment, and half of them are used for each procedure.

Allogeneic stem cell transplant

Here the stem cells do not come from the patient, but from a donor whose tissue type is matched with the patient. The donor may be a family member, usually a sibling. The donor may be sought from a national registry as well. This may be called a MUD (matched unrelated donor) transplant. Cord blood transplant is another method where blood is taken from the placenta and umbilical cord of newborns. This blood has a high number of stem cells. But the number of stem cells in a unit of cord blood is often too low for large adults, so this source of stem cells has so far been used more in children. The advantage of allogenic transplant is that the donor stem cells make their own immune cells, which may help destroy any cancer cells in the patient. The disadvantage is the risk of graft rejection that may require lifelong use of immunity suppressing agents.

What is allogenic stem cell transplant used for?

Allogeneic transplant is most often used to treat certain types of leukemia, lymphomas, and other bone marrow disorders such as myelodysplasia. Many factors play a role in how the immune system knows the difference between "self" and "non-self." The most important factor that is used in allogenic transplants is called human leukocyte antigen (HLA) system. Human leukocyte antigens are proteins found on the surface of most cells. Each person has a number of pairs of HLA antigens (the best-known ones being A, B, C, DR, DQ, and DP). They inherit one of each of these antigens from each of their patents. Doctors try to match these antigens when finding a donor for a person getting a stem cell transplant.

Reviewed by April Cashin-Garbutt, BA Hons (Cantab); Source: http://www.news-medical.net/health/Bone-Marrow-Transplant.aspx

Question 3

From the text it follows that

A) Leukemia cannot be treated with allogeneic BMT
B) Autologous BMT uses matched unrelated donors
C) Syngeneic BMT would not be an option for many people
D) Allogeneic BMT can reintroduce cancer cells into the body

Question 4

It is true that

A) Graft rejection is more likely with allogeneic BMT
B) Graft rejection is not possible with autologous BMT
C) Graft rejection will be less likely if patients have high-dose radiation
D) Graft rejection is a factor in each and every bone marrow transplant

Question 5

The purpose of matching in allogeneic BMT is to

A) Treat the stem cells as "non-self"
B) Use cord blood to overcome the need for immunity suppressing agents
C) Use a registered donor with high levels of HLA
D) Identify the stem cells as "self"

Question 6

In a town of 1,000 people two-fifths are men. Of the women, 230 are not vegan. All of the people drink water and also drink the juices from fresh fruit. The total number of non-vegans is equal to the number of men and 10% of women.

From this information which of the following is true?

A) The total number of non-vegans is equal to the total number of women
B) The number of non-vegan women is the same as the number of non-vegan men.
C) 59% of all of the people are vegan
D) A higher proportion of men are vegan

Question 7

There are 73 coloured marbles in a cloth bag. The marble colours are as follows:

        8 marbles are green
        7 marbles are red
        4 marbles are orange
        8 marbles are blue
        11 marbles are black
        13 marbles are purple
        7 marbles are yellow
        4 marbles are turquoise
        5 marbles are pink
        6 marbles are white

What is the minimum number of marbles that must be taken out of the cloth bag (and not returned to the bag) for a person to be certain that they have drawn out SIX different coloured marbles?

A) 6 marbles
B) 32 marbles
C) 48 marbles
D) 49 marbles

Questions 8 – 10

Myxomatosis is caused by the myxoma virus, a poxvirus spread between rabbits by close contact and biting insects such as fleas and mosquitoes. The virus causes swelling and discharge from the eyes, nose and anogenital region of infected rabbits. Most rabbits die within 10-14 days of infection however highly virulent strains of the myxoma virus may cause death before the usual signs of infection have appeared.

Myxomatosis was introduced to Australia in 1950 to reduce pest rabbit numbers. The virus initially reduced the wild rabbit population by 95% but since then resistance to the virus has increased and less deadly strains of the virus have emerged. Pet rabbits do not possess any resistance to myxomatosis and mortality rates are between 96-100%. With such a poor prognosis treatment is not usually recommended.

There are two vaccinations against myxomatosis, however these are not available in Australia. Thus the only way to prevent infection is to protect your pet rabbits from biting insects such as fleas and mosquitoes. If your pet rabbit does develop myxomatosis, your vet will advise the best course of action, which may be euthanasia. Treatment is rarely successful, even if commenced early in the infection, and the course of disease is very painful and stressful. Bringing a new rabbit home is not recommended for at least four months after a case of myxomatosis as the virus is able to survive in the environment for some time.

Source: http://kb.rspca.org.au/What-is-myxomatosis-and-how-do-I-protect-my-rabbit-from-it_73.html

Question 8

From the information

A) Ninety five percent of rabbits are susceptible to the myxoma virus
B) Pet rabbits in a mosquito-free environment are safe from the myxoma virus
C) A rabbit with myxomatosis should be euthanaised
D) A pet rabbit contracting myxomatosis is highly likely to die

Question 9

It follows that

A) Fleas can catch the myxoma virus from mosquitos
B) A rabbit can die before it shows symptoms of myxomatosis
C) A rabbit with myxomatosis is a danger to other pets
D) The myxoma virus is active even in cold conditions

Question 10

The myxoma vaccine

A) Is limited in availability in order to stop wild rabbits from building resistance
B) Is effective after a rabbit has caught myxomatosis
C) Brings severe pain and stress to rabbits
D) Takes at least four months to be effective

Questions 11 - 12

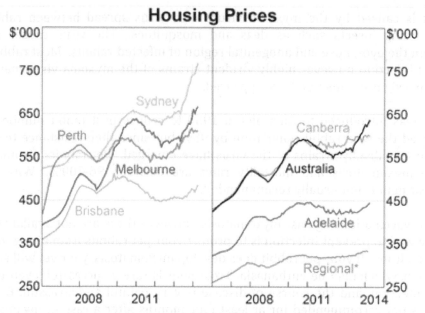

Housing Prices

* Excludes apartments; measured as areas outside of capital cities in mainland states

Sources: RBA; RP Data-Rismark

Source: http://www.rba.gov.au/chart-pack/household-sector.html

Question 11

The city most closely matching the trend in Australian housing prices is

A) Canberra
B) Melbourne
C) Perth
D) Sydney

Question 12

From the graph, which of the following is true?

A) From 2008 – 2011 house prices in Melbourne rose at a faster rate than house prices in Sydney or Canberra
B) From 2010 – 2014 average house prices in Adelaide and Brisbane fell
C) The GFC had a significant effect on housing prices in Australia
D) House prices in regional areas of Australia in 2014 are on average a third of the value of house prices in Sydney

Questions 13 – 15

<u>What is Iliotibial band syndrome (ITBS)?</u>

Iliotibial band syndrome is a condition that commonly presents in runners and typically causes pain at the outer (lateral) aspect of the knee where the iliotibial band (ITB) crosses the knee joint. Iliotibial band syndrome describes a condition whereby the iliotibial band rubs against a bony prominence at the outer aspect of the knee (the femoral epicondyle – Figure 1) and typically causes inflammation and damage to the ITB and local tissue.

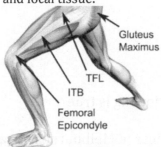

Figure 1 – Relevant Anatomy for Iliotibial Band Syndrome (ITBS)

The iliotibial band is a long band of connective tissue than runs down the outer aspect of the thigh (Figure 1). It originates from two muscles on the outer aspect of the hip (the *tensor fascia latae* (TFL) and *gluteus maximus*) and runs down past the knee to attach into the lower leg bone (tibia). As the ITB crosses the knee, it overlies a bony prominence known as the femoral epicondyle. As the knee bends and straightens the ITB flicks over this bony prominence which places friction on the ITB and local soft tissue. If this friction becomes excessive or too repetitive (such as during excessive running) the ITB or local tissue can become damaged or inflamed resulting in pain. When this occurs the condition is known as Iliotibial Band Syndrome (ITBS).

Any overuse activity which involves repetitive knee bending and straightening, particularly in weight bearing, can contribute to the development of the condition (i.e. walking, running, cycling, rowing). Iliotibial band syndrome (ITBS) is commonly seen in marathon runners, athletes, triathletes and footballers.

Patients with iliotibial band syndrome usually experience pain at the outer aspect of the knee. Patients usually experience an ache that may increase to a sharper pain with activity. Pain is typically experienced during activities that bend or straighten the knee particularly whilst weight bearing. Pain may be worse first thing in the morning or following activity (once the body has cooled down). This may be associated with knee stiffness and can sometimes cause the patient to limp. Activities that frequently aggravate symptoms include running (particularly longer runs, downhill running or running on cambered surfaces), walking (particularly up and down stairs or hills), squatting or jumping. Patients with ITB syndrome typically experience pain when firmly touching the outer aspect of the knee (femoral epicondyle – Figure 1). There are several factors which can predispose patients to developing Iliotibial band syndrome. Some of these factors include:

1. muscle tightness (particularly TFL, *gluteus maximus*, *vastus lateralis* or calf)
2. inadequate recovery periods from sport or activity
3. inadequate warm up
4. inadequate rehabilitation following a previous lower limb injury
5. a sudden change in training volume, intensity, frequency, duration, conditions or surfaces
6. abnormal running biomechanics
7. poor pelvic or core stability

Source: http://www.physioadvisor.com.au/10291450/iliotibial-band-syndrome-iliotibial-syndrome-i.htm

12

Question 13

From the information it can be concluded that

A) Runners who train heavily will get ITBS
B) Skiers would be susceptible to ITBS
C) Walking down stairs can aggravate ITBS
D) Knee stiffness indicates ITBS

Question 14

ITBS occurs when

A) tissue around the ITB becomes inflamed
B) there is damage to the femoral epicondyle
C) there is pain touching the outside of the knee
D) the ITB rubs over the femoral epicondyle

Question 15

Which of the following is _NOT_ a factor that predisposes a person to ITBS?

A) A tight *tensor fascia latae*
B) Asymmetrical running gait
C) Inadequate rehabilitation from a lower limb injury
D) Poor core stability

Questions 16 - 17

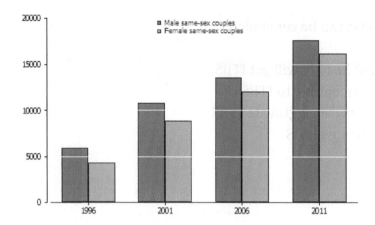

Source: http://www.abs.gov.au/AUSSTATS/abs@.nsf/Lookup/4102.0Main+Features10July+2013

Question 16

From the graph what can be concluded?

A) Social changes have meant that more people feel comfortable disclosing their same sex orientation
B) The rate of increase in same sex male couples is greater than the rate of increase in same sex female couples
C) In 2011 there were 35,000 same sex couples in Australia
D) In 2016 the number of same sex male couples should exceed 20,000

Question 17

Which of the following is true?

A) The proportion of female same sex couples to male same sex couples has increased over time
B) The proportion of female same sex couples to male same sex couples has decreased over time
C) The proportion of female same sex couples to male same sex couples has remained steady over time
D) The proportion of female same sex couples to male same sex couples has increased by 30% over the period 1996 to 2011

Questions 18 - 19

Look at the information in the Table below.

Apothecaries Weight	Avoirdupois Weight
20 grains = 1 scruple	$27\,{}^{11}/_{32}$ grains = 1 drachm
3 scruples = 1 drachm	16 drachms = 1 ounce = 28.35 grams
8 drachms = 1 ounce	16 ounces = 1 pound = 453.59 grams
12 ounces = 1 pound	28 pounds = 1 quarter
	4 quarters = 1 cwt (centrum weight)
1 ounce = 31.10 grams	2,000 pounds = 1 short ton
1 pound = 373.24 grams	2,240 pounds = 1 long ton

Table 1 Data for Apothecaries and Avoirdupois Weight, Note: 1 grain = 0.065grams

Question 18

A pharmacist uses an old set of scales to weigh a bottle of liquid, recording the weight as "80-82 grains".

Which of the following CANNOT be true?

A) The bottle of liquid weighs 1.33 drachm
B) The bottle of liquid weighs 5.2 grams
C) Half a dozen bottles weigh 1 ounce
D) Half a dozen bottles weigh 56.7 grams

Question 19

What is the relationship between Apothecaries Weight and Avoirdupois Weight?

A) There is no relationship between the scales
B) In metric terms, Apothecaries Weight would equate to higher numerical values than Avoirdupois Weight
C) In metric terms, a drachm in Avoirdupois Weight would equate to about twice the Apothecaries Weight
D) 16 ounces under both systems of measurement equates to 453.59 grams

The False ADHD Controversy

More kids are being diagnosed with attention deficit hyperactivity disorder (ADHD) than ever before, according to the Centers for Disease Control. 8.8% of children were diagnosed in 2011, compared with 7.0% in 2007. An uptick was also witnessed in the number of parents choosing to medicate their children with stimulants such as Ritalin. That proportion now sits at two-thirds.

ADHD is perhaps childhood's most common neurobehavioral disorder. It's characterised by an array of symptoms, including squirming, excessive daydreaming, forgetfulness, and hyperactivity. Scientists still can't precisely pinpoint what's going on in the brain to trigger ADHD, but it's evident that something is amiss. Children with ADHD generally have reduced brain volume in the left pre-frontal cortex.

But the lack of a conclusive causal mechanism in the brain leads many onlookers to conclude that ADHD is a manufactured condition. Its symptoms are merely side effects of childhood, they argue. But this is not in agreement with evidence stemming from genetics. Thanks to large twin studies, a number of genes have been implicated, particularly those that affect dopamine transporters. The dopamine system of the brain regulates a whole heap of processes, but it's most commonly linked with reward seeking. As far as ADHD goes, we know that when dopamine levels are driven up within the brain, ADHD symptoms lessen in severity.

ADHD certainly exists, says Russell Barkley, a professor of psychiatry and neurology at the University of Massachusetts.

"No scientific meetings mention any controversies about the disorder, about its validity as a disorder, about the usefulness of using stimulant medications like Ritalin for it. There simply is no controversy. The science speaks for itself. And the science is overwhelming that the answer to these questions is in the affirmative: it's a real disorder; it's valid; and it can be managed, in many cases, by using stimulant medication in combination with other treatments."

There are legitimate realms of disagreement over ADHD, however. The fact that kids in North Carolina are twice as likely to be diagnosed with the disorder than kids in California shows that there must be more at work than genetics. Environmental factors like parenting, economic status, diet, and exposure to cigarette smoking may also play minor roles. Moreover, the fact that Britain has rates of ADHD less than half that of the United States likely shows that Americans are more apt to diagnose - or over diagnose - it.

Even more contentious is the question of when to use medications like Ritalin or Adderall, which - like cocaine, amphetamines, and opium - are classified by the Drug Enforcement Agency as schedule II controlled substances. Is it really wise to be placing children on such drug regimens, especially when their brains are still in the sensitive process of developing? That's for parents to decide, but general scientific consensus seems to point to "yes." In cases of ADHD where dietary and behavioural modifications don't seem to cut it, medication can be a life-changer.

"The judicious use of medication... is a good idea," Max Wiznitizer a pediatric neurologist at Case Western Reserve University, told ABC News. "The goal of the medication is to help kids focus, to reduce their impulsivity, and also to allow them to function adequately in their social environment."

Those who blatantly deny the existence of ADHD or blindly oppose the drugs to treat it often don't consider the consequences for children who don't receive appropriate care. One study found that they're more likely to drop out of school and be unsuccessful later in life.

Source: Stephen Ross Pomeroy from http://www.forbes.com/sites/rosspomeroy/2013/12/16/the-false-adhd-controversy/

Question 20

Attention hyperactivity deficit disorder (ADHD)

A) is an experience children have, not an independently observable phenomenon
B) manifests as small brains, reward seeking behaviour and squirming
C) is observable but not independently validated
D) is associated with inadequate social functioning

Question 21

From the text it follows that Ritalin

A) overcomes symptoms of childhood
B) increases dopamine levels
C) is as harmful to the brain as amphetamines
D) is required to help children overcome their impulsivity

Question 22

I   The flight of a ball when struck by a bat or club is not parabolic as drag reduces the horizontal speed of a ball in flight late in its trajectory.

II   A spinning ball will travel higher and further given the same impetus.

III   A dimpled ball gets more lift and travels further given the same impetus.

IV   A ball hit on the underside will fly with backspin and gets greater height given the same impetus.

V   A ball hit with overspin or top spin will fly lower and bounce further given the same impetus.

The pictures below represent which of the five types of flight?

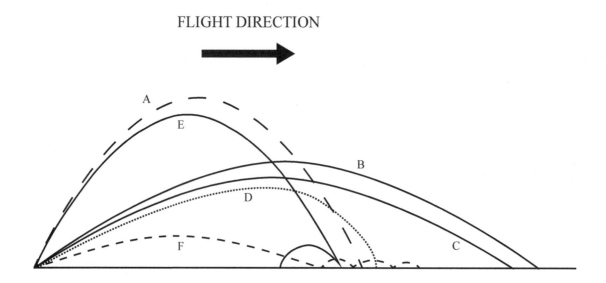

FLIGHT DIRECTION

A) A = I, B = II, C = III, D = V, F = IV
B) A = IV, B = III, C = I, E = V, F = II
C) B = III, C = II, D = I, E = V, F = IV
D) B = III, C = II, D = I, E = IV, F = V

Questions 23 - 24

To stay warm when temperatures drop outside, we heat our indoor spaces - even when no one is in them. But scientists have now developed a novel nanowire coating for clothes that can both generate heat and trap the heat from our bodies better than regular clothes.

Yi Cui and colleagues note that nearly half of global energy consumption goes toward heating buildings and homes. But this comfort comes with a considerable environmental cost - it's responsible for up to a third of the world's total greenhouse gas emissions. Scientists and policymakers have tried to reduce the impact of indoor heating by improving insulation and construction materials to keep fuel-generated warmth inside. Cui's team wanted to take a different approach and focus on people rather than spaces.

The researchers developed lightweight, breathable mesh materials that are flexible enough to coat normal clothes. When compared to regular clothing material, the special nanowire cloth trapped body heat far more effectively. Because the coatings are made out of conductive materials, they can also be actively warmed with an electricity source to further crank up the heat. The researchers calculated that their thermal textiles could save about 1,000 kilowatt hours per person every year - that's about how much electricity an average U.S. home consumes in one month.

Journal Reference: Po-Chun Hsu, Xiaoge Liu, Chong Liu, Xing Xie, Hye Ryoung Lee, Alex J. Welch, Tom Zhao, Yi Cui. **Personal Thermal Management by Metallic Nanowire-Coated Textile**. *Nano Letters*, 2014; 141203091130001 DOI: 10.1021/nl5036572 from http://www.sciencedaily.com/releases/2015/01/150107122914.htm, *Source:* American Chemical Society, 7/1/15

Question 23

From the text it follows that

A) nanowire fibres will be the substance used in future clothing design
B) greenhouse gas emissions will be reduced through the use of nanowire clothing
C) the management of heating is a significant concern for scientists
D) warming people is more effective that warming buildings

Question 24

Development of nanowire coated clothing will most likely take place when

A) the environmental costs rise to high levels
B) the cost of manufacture is much lower that the costs of heating
C) half of the world's energy costs rise too high
D) the U.S finds the costs of heating and cooling unsustainable

Coughing probably doesn't seem like a big deal in your day-to-day life. You feel the urge to cough, and then you cough. You probably don't even think about it because it's second nature. However, that may change after having surgery. Coughing is not nearly as easy when you are recovering after a procedure, and it certainly isn't painless, either.

Why Is Coughing Important After Surgery?

After surgery, coughing is essential for preventing pneumonia and keeping the lungs clear. Many patients avoid coughing because it can be very painful; however, it is imperative that you cough enough to prevent lung complications. For patients who avoid coughing, or are too weak to cough, it may be necessary to provide assistance in keeping the lungs clear. In the hospital, suction can be used to assist patients with keeping their lungs clear; however, coughing is much more effective and preferable to suction.

How To Cough After Surgery

When you feel the urge to cough, you should brace your incision if you have a chest or abdominal surgical site. That means taking your hands or a small pillow and hugging it to your incision when you cough, applying gentle but firm pressure. If your incision is on your chest, such as after an open heart surgery, you would hug a pillow to your chest directly over your incision. If your incision is on your abdomen, you would hug a pillow to your abdominal incision. If no pillow is available, you can use your hands to brace the incision, as the pillow is primarily for comfort. Even if your incision is not on your chest or abdomen, bracing may help with pain control.

Why You Should Brace Your Incision When Coughing

Bracing your incision is very important for several reasons. Holding pressure on your incision while you cough decreases the stress on it, which can significantly decrease the pain you feel. In addition, the support you give your incision can prevent it from pulling apart and opening, a complication called dehiscence, which can become very serious.

How To Cough and Deep Breathe

Coughing and deep breathing is a technique used to help keep the lungs clear during the first few days after surgery. The technique varies slightly between facilities and physicians, but the general idea is the same.

- Take a deep breath, hold it for several seconds, and then slowly let it out.
- Repeat step one five times.
- Brace your incision and attempt to cough deeply.
- Repeat every 1-2 hours.

Sneezing After Surgery

The idea is the same with sneezing as it is with coughing - bracing will protect your incision and help minimise the pain you feel. Never stifle a sneeze; holding one in can be far more painful than just letting it happen naturally.

Source: http://surgery.about.com/od/aftersurgery/a/How-To-Coughing-After-Surgery.htm

Question 25

Coughing after chest surgery

A) prevents pneumonia and emphysema
B) is painful and should be avoided
C) should be encouraged, as should sneezing
D) can help clear the lungs and can damage the incision

Question 26

From the text, it should follow that

A) pillows assist in recovery from open heart surgery
B) holding the breath is appropriate for recovery from open heart surgery
C) every 1–2 hours patients should brace themselves to relieve pressure on stitches
D) abdominal surgery encourages sneezing and coughing

Questions 27 - 28

Vital teeth bleaching

There are three fundamental approaches for bleaching vital teeth: in-office or power bleaching, at-home or dentist-supervised night-guard bleaching, and bleaching with over-the-counter (OTC) products (Kihn, 2007).

First, in-office bleaching utilises a high concentration of tooth-whitening agents (25–40% hydrogen peroxide). Here, the dentist has complete control throughout the procedure and has the ability to stop it when the desired shade/effect is achieved. In this procedure, the whitening gel is applied to the teeth after protection of the soft tissues by rubber dam or alternatives (Powell and Bales, 1991), and the peroxide will further be activated (or not) by heat or light for around one hour in the dental office (Sulieman, 2004). Different types of curing lights including: halogen curing lights, Plasma arc lamp, Xe–halogen light (Luma Arch), Diode lasers (both 830 and 980 nm wavelength diode lasers), or Metal halide (Zoom) light can be used to activate the bleaching gel or accelerate the whitening effect.

Second, at-home or dentist-supervised night-guard bleaching basically involves the use of a low concentration of whitening agent (10–20% carbamide peroxide, which equals 3.5–6.5% hydrogen peroxide). In general, it is recommended that the 10% carbamide peroxide be used 8 h per day, and the 15–20% carbamide peroxide 3–4 h per day. This treatment is carried out by the patients themselves, but it should be supervised by dentists during recall visits.

The at-home technique offers many advantages: self-administration by the patient, less chair-side time, high degree of safety, fewer adverse effects, and low cost. Despite the fact that patients are able to bleach at their own pace, this at-home bleaching technique, with its various concentrations of bleaching materials and regimens, has become the gold standard by which other techniques are judged. However, it is by no means without disadvantages, since active patient compliance is mandatory and the technique suffers from high dropout rates (Leonard et al., 2003). In addition, colour change is dependent on diligence of use, and the results are sometimes less than ideal, since some patients do not remember to wear the trays every day. In contrast, excessive use by overzealous patients is also possible, which frequently causes thermal sensitivity, reported to be as high as 67% (Haywood, 1992).

Finally, over-the-counter (OTC) bleaching products have increased in popularity in recent years. These products are composed of a low concentration of whitening agent (3–6% hydrogen peroxide) and are self-applied to the teeth via gum shields, strips, or paint-on product formats. They are also available as whitening dentifrices, pre-fabricated trays, whitening strips, and toothpastes (Zantner et al., 2007). They should be applied twice per day for up to 2 weeks. OTC products are considered to be the fastest growing sector of the dental market (Kugel, 2003). However, these bleaching agents may be of highly questionable safety, because some are not regulated by the Food and Drug Administration.

Source: Tooth-bleaching procedures and their controversial effects: A literature review, by Mohammed Q. Alqahtani, from: http://www.saudidentaljournal.com/article/S1013-9052(14)00018-2/abstract?cc=y

Question 27

From the information it can be concluded that

A) curing lights are necessary for effective bleaching
B) colour change always will carry side effects
C) patients closely following the prescribed at-home regime should have success
D) thermal sensitivity follows the use of bleaching agents

Question 28

A medium concentration of hydrogen peroxide in a whitening agent would equate to

A) 7%
B) 18%
C) 24%
D) 38%

Question 29

A woman with brunette hair and a woman with black hair are discussing travel options as they sip chai latte. The brunette haired woman states, "I love travelling north." The black haired woman replies, "I love travelling south." It is known that one of the women loves travelling north and one loves travelling south. At least one of the women is lying.

Which of the following is correct?

    A) The brunette haired woman is telling the truth
    B) The black haired woman cannot be lying
    C) Both of the women are lying
    D) The brunette haired woman loves travelling south

NUTRITION INFORMATION SERVINGS PER PACKAGE: 8.8 SERVING SIZE: 25g (approx. 4 squares)	AVG QTY PER SERVING	% DAILY INTAKE* PER SERVING	AVG. QTY PER 100g
ENERGY	559kJ	6%	2,240kJ
PROTEIN	2.0g	4%	8.1g
FAT – TOTAL	7.4g	11%	29.6g
- SATURATED	4.7g	20%	18.7g
CARBOHYDRATE	14.8g	5%	59.1g
- SUGARS	14.3g	16%	57.3g
SODIUM	22mg	1%	87mg

*Percentage Daily Intakes (PDIs) are based on an average adult diet of 8,700kJ (2,080 calories). Your daily intakes may be higher or lower depending on your energy needs

Question 30

A PDI of 16% for protein would equate to eating how many squares of the product?

A) 1
B) 2
C) 4
D) 16

Question 31

How many packages of product would a person need to consume in order to just achieve the Calorie equivalence of the average adult?

A) 1
B) 2
C) 2½
D) 2¾

Questions 32 - 33

Distance (m)	Year for Projected World Record Times Men's running events (hr:min:sec.hundredths)			
	2000	**2028**	**2040**	**Ultimate**
100	9.74	9.57	9.49	9.37
200	19.53	19.10	18.92	18.32
400	43.44	42.12	41.59	39.60
800	1:39.88	1:36.18	1:34.71	1:30.86
1,000	2:09.72	2:04.81	2:02.86	1:57.53
3,000	7:22.54	7:03.91	6:56.87	6:24.81
5,000	12:42.72	12:09.39	11:56.19	11:11.61
10,000	26:43.63	25:52.27	25:04.01	23:36.89
21,100	59:55.03	57:11.96	56:07.38	52:20.03
42,195	2:05:23.72	1:59:36.08	1:57:18.47	1:48:25.25

From: Peronnet and Thibault (1989, pg 463) cited in Tim Noakes, Lore of Running (4th Ed), p691

Distance (m)	Actual World Record Times At January 2015 (hr:min:sec.hundredths)
100	9.58 by Usain Bolt (Aug 2009)
200	19.19 by Usain Bolt (Aug 2009)
400	43.18 by Michael Johnson (Aug 1999)
800	1:40.91 by David Lekuta Rudisha (Aug 2012)
1,000	2:11.96 by Noah Ngeny (Sept 1999)
3,000	7:20.67 by Daniel Komen (Sept 1996)
5,000	12:37.35 by Kenenisa Bekele (May 2004)
10,000	26:44 by Leonard Patrick Komon (Sept 2010)
21,100	58:23 by Zersenay Tadese (March 2010)
42,195	2:02:57 by Dennis Kipruto Kimetto (Sept 2014)

Source: International Association of Amateur Athletics from http://www.iaaf.org/records/by-category/world-records

Question 32

From the data above it can be concluded that

A) On the shortest distances record times are significantly lower than projected times
B) On the longest distances record times are significantly lower than projected times
C) There is no correlation between projected times and actual world record times
D) World records will meet projected times faster than predicted

Question 33

From the data it follows that

A) the projected times for 800m and 10,000m will never be achieved
B) most world athletic events are held in the second half of the year
C) improvements in training and diet should lower the world record times
D) the 3,000m world record will not be broken any time soon

Question 34

Select the alternative that most logically and simply continues the series.

521525   46614   7293   842

A) 21
B) 111
C) 11
D) 12
E) 421

Question 35

In the country of Facto, Lago is bigger than Ohno. Jolo is smaller than Nogo. Ipso is not a town in Facto. Additional information is as follows:

    I)   Lago is smaller than Uboo
    II)   Ipso is a large nation
    III) Nogo is the largest town
    IV) There is one town larger than Uboo
    V)   If Ipso was in Facto it would be the largest town
    VI) There is one town smaller than Jolo
    VII) Ohno is not the largest town

Which of the statements taken together prove that Lago is bigger than Jolo and smaller than Nogo?

A) I, III, IV and VI only
B) I, II, III and VII only
C) III, IV, VI and VII only
D) III, IV, V and VI only

Questions 36 - 37

What do scientists know about the ingredients in antiperspirants and deodorants?

Aluminum-based compounds are used as the active ingredient in antiperspirants. These compounds form a temporary plug within the sweat duct that stops the flow of sweat to the skin's surface. Some research suggests that aluminum-based compounds, which are applied frequently and left on the skin near the breast, may be absorbed by the skin and cause estrogen-like (hormonal) effects. Because estrogen has the ability to promote the growth of breast cancer cells, some scientists have suggested that the aluminum-based compounds in antiperspirants may contribute to the development of breast cancer.

Some research has focused on parabens, which are preservatives used in some deodorants and antiperspirants that have been shown to mimic the activity of estrogen in the body's cells. Although parabens are used in many cosmetic, food, and pharmaceutical products, according to the FDA, most major brands of deodorants and antiperspirants in the United States do not currently contain parabens. Consumers can look at the ingredient label to determine if a deodorant or antiperspirant contains parabens. Parabens are usually easy to identify by name, such as methylparaben, propylparaben, butylparaben, or benzylparaben.

Source: http://www.cancer.gov/cancertopics/factsheet/Risk/AP-Deo

---

Question 36

It can be concluded that

A) aluminium causes the growth of cancer cells
B) antiperspirants kill the bacteria that causes odour from sweating
C) parabens and aluminium make similar compounds
D) butylparaben will copy the activity of estrogen in male body cells

Question 37

It follows that researchers should

A) explore the possible link between aluminium and breast cancer
B) develop aluminium-free products
C) find a means to remove aluminium from breast tissue
D) develop estrogen-reducing drugs

Question 38

$$1 + 2 + 3 + 4 + 5 + 6 + \ldots\ldots + 199 + 200 + 201 = \ ?$$

A) 20,001
B) 20,201
C) 20,301
D) 20,401

Questions 39 - 40

Debt compared with assets

Rising household debt has been only partly matched by the increase in the value of household assets. Over the past 25 years, household debt has increased nearly twice as fast as the value of household assets. Expressed as a percentage of the value of household assets, household debt increased from just under 11% at the end of September 1988 to nearly 21% at the end of 2011, before easing a little to below 20% at the end of 2013.

SIZE OF HOUSEHOLD DEBT COMPARED WITH ASSETS (a)

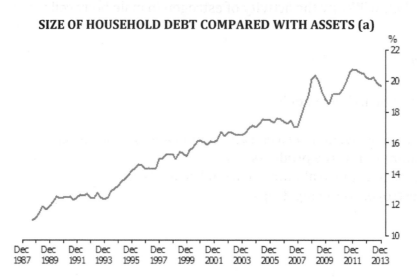

Source: Australian National Accounts: Financial Accounts, December Quarter 2013 (ABS cat. no. 5232.0)

Debt compared with income

Income is an important consideration when deciding on a household's capacity to make loan repayments in full and on time. Household debt increased more rapidly than household income from early in 1993 until the middle of 2007. Since mid-2007 (and the GFC), household debt has tended to rise in line with household income. At the end of 2013, the amount that households owed was nearly 1.8 times the amount of disposable income households received during 2013.

SIZE OF HOUSEHOLD DEBT COMPARED WITH ANNUAL INCOME (a)(b)

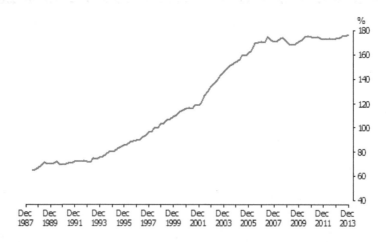

Source: Australian National Accounts: Financial Accounts, December Quarter 2013 (ABS cat. no. 5232.0); Australian National Accounts: National Income, Expenditure and Product, December Quarter 2013 (ABS cat. no. 5206.0)

Question 39

From the data provided it can be reliably concluded that

A) throughout the period December 1987 to December 2013 the size of household debt increased steadily and predictably

B) the average household debt compared to assets over the period December 1987 to December 2013 was 16.4%

C) the highest rate of growth in size of household debt was between December 2007 and June 2009

D) the GFC was responsible for the fall in household debt in December 2007 and December 2009

Question 40

From the data provided it follows that

A) household income and the value of household assets closely correlate

B) from December 2006 annual income has not really increased at all

C) if a person applied all of their income to debt from the end of 2013 it would take until mid-October 2015 to pay it all off

D) people have become more risk averse over time

Question 41

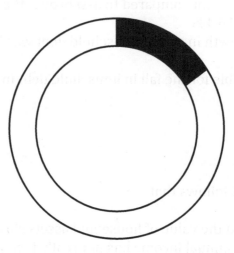

■ Ischaemic heart disease (IHD)

Proportion of all deaths

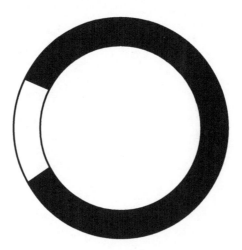

Deaths from heart disease

Question 41

Together these two diagrams indicate that

A) ischaemic heart disease is more likely to cause death than other types of disease
B) ischaemic heart disease causes about 15% of deaths due to heart disease
C) ischaemic heart disease makes up just over 15% of deaths yet is responsible for over 85% of deaths from heart diseases
D) deaths from all types of heart disease are nearly six times as common as deaths resulting from ischaemic heart disease

Question 42 - 43

The world's leading medical experts say antibiotic resistance now poses a serious threat to global health.

The World Health Organisation's (WHO) first worldwide report into antimicrobial resistance has found the problem is no longer just a serious prediction for the future, but is happening now. The report says as well as superbugs in hospitals, everyday infections such as pneumonia and urinary tract infections are becoming harder to treat. In Australia there are high levels of E. coli resistance to an important and commonly used antibiotic, fluoroquinolones, and widespread resistance to drugs used to treat pneumonia and bloodstream infections. In some parts of the country, 80 per cent of staph infections cannot be treated with standard antibiotics. The report makes a clear case that resistance to common bacteria has reached alarming levels in many parts of the world, indicating that several of the available treatment options for common infections are becoming ineffective.

What is antibiotic resistance?

Antibiotic or antimicrobial resistance occurs when microorganisms such as bacteria, viruses, fungi and parasites change in ways that render the medications used to cure the infections they cause ineffective. When the microorganisms become resistant to most antimicrobials, they are often referred to as superbugs.

Source: Antibiotic resistance poses a worldwide threat to human health: World Health Organisation, By medical reporter Sophie Scott

Dr Keiji Fukuda, assistant director-general for health security at the WHO, says a systematic review of the scientific evidence shows that antibiotic resistance has a negative impact on outcomes for patients and healthcare expenditures.

"Generally, surveillance in tuberculosis, malaria and HIV to detect resistance, determine disease burden and monitor public health interventions is better established and experiences from these programs are described in the report, so that lessons learnt can be applied to antibiotic resistance and opportunities for collaboration identified," he said.

The report is the beginning of a global effort by the WHO to address drug resistance. It will involve the development of tools and improved collaboration around the world to track drug resistance, measure its impact, and design solutions.

"Strengthening global surveillance will be a critical aspect of such planning as it is the basis for informing global strategies, monitoring the effectiveness of public health interventions and detecting new trends and threats," the report says.

Professor Peter Collignon from the Australian National University says many of the superbugs are being brought into Australia when people return from holidays.

"It's really important if anyone is having surgery to let their doctors know if they have travelled in the last six to 12 months," he said.

Source: http://www.abc.net.au/news/2014-05-01/antibiotic-resistance-poses-threat-to-global-health-who-report/5422080

Question 42

Research indicates that use of antibiotics

A) should be stopped in treatment as it creates antimicrobial resistance
B) needs to be reassessed through close monitoring
C) is ineffective in the treatment of pneumonia
D) has been increasingly of little effectiveness against bacteria

Question 43

In Australia

A) superbugs come from resistance to antibiotics and from people travelling offshore
B) 80% of staph infections cannot be treated with standard antibiotics
C) bloodstream infections are on the increase
D) urinary tract infections cannot be effectively treated

Questions 44 – 46

Scientists are developing robots smaller than the width of a human hair with the idea they could be controlled on a molecular level - that's literally moving atoms and cells us humans aren't able to. They could be programmed and put to use inside human bodies to tinker around with the smallest of our cells, be part of a million-strong miniature work force for rapid construction or even be used as a potential weapon.

The application of nanotechnology in the field of medicine is possibly the most exciting and life-changing prospect. It has doctors and potential patients fizzing with excitement. Research is on going to develop nanobots that could be injected into our bodies to intelligently destroy disease and perform surgeries on individual cells we otherwise couldn't. The cure for cancer could lie with these bots with trials underway using nanoparticles that seek and destroy cancerous cells but without harming surrounding healthy tissue like chemotherapy does.

We may never get sick in the future thanks to nanobot maintained immune systems. It would see the mini machines constantly monitoring you from the inside, pre-empting illness and performing the necessary actions like delivering drugs to keep you tip top. For instance if a cold virus is detected, bots could actively breakdown the very atoms of the virus' molecule.

Medics are hoping nanobots might be the answer to a quicker way to administer medicine into the body as they can be programmed to go straight to the target area. The US defence agency DARPA is developing its In Vivo Nanoplatform program to help diagnose and rapidly treat disease within soldiers, perhaps eliminating the need for medics on the frontline as the drug-carrying bots could be self-delivered. Elsewhere in medicine we are turning to nanobots to help in brain surgery thanks to their ability to manoeuvre their micron size through the complex and delicate passageways.

Nanotech pioneer Robert Freitas has designed a bot called a Respirocyte that can carry 9 billion oxygen and carbon dioxide molecules — 200 times that of typical red blood cells — meaning that humans could run at full tilt for a good 15 minutes without running out of puff. The same level ability to hold oxygen means we could also go without having to take a breath for hours. As well as this super stamina, muscle tissue could be broken down by bots and re-worked to give us super strength, poor eyesight could be rectified and teeth kept clean to microscopic levels. Nanobots could be programmed to seek out ageing cells, tissue and muscles that have lost any ability due to degeneration for repair, replace and tune up. It means we could essentially extend lifespan and keep razor-sharp well into old age.

If you're still wary of nanorobotics just think what they could do for the environment. A disaster like an oil spill takes an extraordinary level of effort to clean, if fully cleaned at all. But nanobots deployed at the scene could get scrubbing in their millions, destroying every contaminated molecule much faster than any method currently available. In smog-ridden cities or chemical emitting factories a swarm released into the atmosphere could deconstruct the pollutants. Safe, purified drinking water without the need for chemicals could be made available anywhere with nanotechnology particles destroying the water-borne bacteria, which claims many lives.

Source: James Billington, "The mind-blowing things nanobots could do", from:
http://www.news.com.au/technology/gadgets/the-mind-blowing-things-nanobots-could-do/story-fnpjxpz3-1227166669101

Question 44

Nanobots

A) are tiny, cellular organisms that kill cancer cells
B) can be used to clean impure drinking water in smog filled cities
C) are being designed but have not yet been developed
D) can hold two hundred times more oxygen than red blood cells

Question 45

It can be concluded that

A) the use of nanobots will eliminate the need for doctors
B) nanobots will help people to live up to five years longer
C) nanobots will give people the stamina needed to live longer
D) nanobots may be programmed to distinguish cancer cells from normal cells

Question 46

It follows that

A) nanotechnology has uses beyond the field of medicine
B) the size of nanobots must be molecular for medical success
C) the most effective nanorobots will work in the respiratory system
D) toothpaste will be phased out through the use of nanobots

Ebola Virus Disease

Ebola virus disease (EVD), formerly known as Ebola haemorrhagic fever, is a severe, often fatal illness to humans. The virus is transmitted to people from wild animals and spreads in the human population through human-to-human transmission. The average EVD case fatality rate is around 50%. Case fatality rates have ranged from 25% to 90% in past outbreaks.

It is thought that fruit bats of the Pteropodidae family are natural Ebola virus hosts. Ebola is introduced into the human population through close contact with the blood, secretions, organs or other bodily fluids of infected animals such as chimpanzees, gorillas, fruit bats, monkeys, forest antelope and porcupines found ill or dead in the forest.

Ebola then spreads through human-to-human transmission via direct contact (through broken skin or mucous membranes) with the blood, secretions, organs or other bodily fluids of infected people, and with surfaces and materials (eg bedding and clothing) contaminated with these fluids.

Health-care workers have frequently been infected while treating patients with suspected or confirmed EVD. This has occurred through close contact with patients when infection control precautions are not strictly practiced. Burial ceremonies in which mourners have direct contact with the body of the deceased person can also play a role in the transmission of Ebola. People remain infectious as long as their blood and body fluids, including semen and breast milk, contain the virus.

The incubation period, that is, the time interval from infection with the virus to onset of symptoms is 2 to 21 days. Humans are not infectious until they develop symptoms. First symptoms are the sudden onset of fever fatigue, muscle pain, headache and sore throat. This is followed by vomiting, diarrhoea, rash, symptoms of impaired kidney and liver function, and in some cases, both internal and external bleeding (e.g. oozing from the gums, blood in the stools). Laboratory findings include low white blood cell and platelet counts and elevated liver enzymes.

It can be difficult to distinguish EVD from other infectious diseases such as malaria, typhoid fever and meningitis. Confirmation that symptoms are caused by Ebola virus infection are made using the following investigations:

1. antibody-capture enzyme-linked immunosorbent assay (ELISA)
2. antigen-capture detection tests
3. serum neutralization test
4. reverse transcriptase polymerase chain reaction (RT-PCR) assay
5. electron microscopy
6. virus isolation by cell culture.

Samples from patients are an extreme biohazard risk; laboratory testing on non-inactivated samples should be conducted under maximum biological containment conditions.

Source: WHO Fact Sheet No 103, Sept 2014, from http://www.who.int/mediacentre/factsheets/fs103/en/

Question 47

It can be concluded

A) a person contracting Ebola virus disease will die
B) twenty two days from infection a person can be infectious
C) people should not touch chimpanzees, gorillas, fruit bats or monkeys
D) blood oozing from the gums is the diagnosis for Ebola

Question 48

It follows that

A) a person bitten by a fruit bat will probably catch Ebola
B) health care workers are at high risk of contracting the virus
C) laboratory technicians should assume all samples they test are Ebola infected
D) contact with the body of a person who died from Ebola can lead to infection

ANSWERS
Summary & Worked Solutions
Multiple Choice Answer Sheet

Logical Reasoning and Problem Solving Answers

1	B	**17**	A	**33**	B
2	C	**18**	D	**34**	B
3	C	**19**	C	**35**	A
4	A	**20**	D	**36**	D
5	D	**21**	B	**37**	A
6	B	**22**	D	**38**	C
7	C	**23**	C	**39**	C
8	D	**24**	B	**40**	C
9	B	**25**	D	**41**	C
10	A	**26**	B	**42**	D
11	B	**27**	C	**43**	A
12	A	**28**	B	**44**	C
13	C	**29**	C	**45**	D
14	A	**30**	D	**46**	A
15	B	**31**	B	**47**	B
16	C	**32**	A	**48**	D

© Mohan Dhall
© Five Senses Education Pty Ltd

Answers

Question 1

B

This pattern is based on the difference between successive (or consecutive) prime numbers. Consider the prime numbers under forty: 2, 3, 5, 7, 11, 13, 17, 19, 23, 29, 31 and 37. In order, the difference between the consecutive prime numbers is: 1, 2, 2, 4, 2, 4, 2, 4, 6, 2 and 6.

Thus B is correct.

Question 2

C

The pattern here is that after the first two numbers each number is the quotient of the previous two numbers. Thus, 3 is 12 divided by 4. The next number, 1.33 is 4 divided by 3. Next is 3 divided by 1.33 which is 2.25. When 1.33 is divided by 2.25 the quotient is 0.59.

Hence the answer is C.

Question 3

C

As syngeneic BMT is only available for people with an identical twin then it follows that this option would be available only to very few people.

Question 4

A

B is patently untrue as in the second paragraph states that there is a 'decreased risk' of rejection, not at no risk. The purpose of high-dose radiation is to kills the cancers, not address the issue of graft rejection, thus C is incorrect. There is no evidence in the text to support D.

Graft rejection can occur in both autologous and allogeneic BMT however is more likely to occur in allogeneic transplants. The text specifically refers to this in paragraph 1 – hence A is correct.

Question 5

D

A is patently incorrect as the purpose of matching is to try and obtain the closest match possible so that the body does not reflect the graft. That is, a close match may help the body to identify the transplant as 'self' and thus not reject it. As regards cord blood – it is a source of stem cells but these cells can still be rejected.

C is not correct, as it is not the levels of HLA but rather the matching of the antigens that matters.

Question 6

B

There are 1,000 people and 2/5 are men (400 men). This means that 600 are women. If 230 are not vegan then it follows that 370 women are vegan. The total number of non-vegans is equal to the number of men (400) and 10% of women (60). This means that there are 460 non-vegans, 230 of whom are women. This means that 230 are also men. Hence B is correct.

Since there are 460 vegans then A is incorrect as there are 600 women. As 540 people in total are vegan (or 54% of the total) then C is incorrect. In terms of proportions: 370 women out of 600 are vegan (61.7%). 170 men out of 400 are vegan (or 42.5%) hence D is also incorrect.

Question 7

C

The answer is 13 + 11 + 8 + 8 + 7 + 1 = 48. Though it would be extremely unlikely, the colours have to be exhausted in order from highest number of one colour to colour with the sixth most prevalence. Hence, all the purple have to be drawn, followed by black, then blue or green (but both have to be drawn) followed by either all of the red or yellow. If all the red marbles are drawn then the 48th marble must be yellow. If all the yellow marbles are drawn then the 48th marble must be red.

Question 8

D

There is nothing in the text to support the conclusion in A, despite the disease killing 95% of the population when introduced. As the disease can be transmitted a number of ways, including through fleas, B cannot be correct. It is possible for a rabbit to survive the disease thus C is not appropriate. Mortality rates are very high, thus D is correct.

Question 9

B

A is patently incorrect. C cannot be a conclusion drawn from the text, as there is no indication that the virus would affect other animals. D is not relevant. B is stated in the text and is thus correct.

Question 10

A

There is nothing to indicate B. The text makes no reference to how rabbits are affected by the vaccine, thus C cannot be correct. There is no indication as to how long it would take the vaccine to work, hence D is incorrect. A can be deduced as the issue of resistance in rabbits would be of concern (and was the impetus for bringing in the disease) and, furthermore, with rabbits showing resistance then the limitation would be both consistent with the text and appropriate.

Question 11

B

Whilst it might, at first glance, appear as though Canberra matches the Australia-wide trend this is not true. Looking closely at the actual shape of each trend line indicates that the most close matching of the trend as it rises and falls actually vests with Melbourne (look very closely at the nuances of the rises and falls ☺)

Question 12

A

The gradient of the slope of the line indicating the trend in Melbourne house prices shows that house prices in that city rose faster there in the period 2008 – 2011 than anywhere else in the nation.

Question 13

C

There is no evidence to indicate A. Some people who over train may get ITBS but that does not mean all runners who train heavily will get it. Moreover, there is no evidence in the information to suggest that skiers would be susceptible. As regards knee stiffness – it can be associated with ITBS but does not mean a person has ITBS. C is correct and is stated in the fourth paragraph.

Question 14

A

ITBS occurs when the rubbing of the ITB against the femoral epicondyle causes inflammation and damage to the ITB – not the epicondyle. Thus B can be discounted. It should be clear that pain can result from more than ITBS (eg bumping the leg against a car door or street light as attention is diverted by a mobile phone or taking of a selfie!) thus C is not correct. The normal working of the knee requires that the ITB rub over the femoral epicondyle – thus this is not ITBS. ITBS occurs when the ITB and surrounding tissue becomes inflamed Thus D is not correct but A is correct.

Question 15

B

Each of A, C and D is listed in the text (see numbers 1-7 at the bottom of the extract. A is found in 1, C is found in 4 and 7 is found in D. Whilst 'abnormal running biomechanics' (6) is stated it is not clear whether this includes as asymmetrical running gait (which is probably actually natural).

Question 16

C

The graph does not give qualitative information to make the conclusion found in A, hence A must be ruled out. The closeness of the columns over time suggests that the rate of increase is at best similar or lower for same sex male couples, hence B is incorrect. No accurate prediction can be made based on this data, hence D is not correct. C can be determined by adding the two columns in 2011 together – hence C is correct.

Question 17

A

As the two columns rise over time the proportions must rise if the difference in height is fairly constant. Thus, only A can be correct.

Question 18

D

Taking A first: "80-82" grains on the Apothecaries Weight Scale would be akin to 4 scruples. 4 scruples is 1.33 drachms, hence A is possible. Now to B: On the Avoirdupois Weight Scale 80-82 grains is 3 drachms or just under 1/5th of an ounce. This would equate to 5.3 grams. On the Apothecaries Weight Scale the bottle would be 1.33/8 of an ounce or 5.17 grams. Thus this answer is also plausible. Using the Apothecaries Weight Scale it follows that half a dozen bottles would be very close in weight to 1 ounce (just over 31 grams). Hence C is also plausible. Since C is true, D cannot be, and in any case even for the Avoirdupois Weight Scale, 6 bottles (half a dozen) weighs about 32 grams. Hence D cannot be true.

Question 19

C

If any of B, C or D is true, then A cannot be true. Though the scales are not identical they do appear to correlate somewhat. B is too general to hold true and D is patently incorrect as an ounce in the Apothecaries Weight Scale is 31.10 grams, whereas it is 28.35 grams in the Avoirdupois Scale.

As regards C: a drachm on Apothecaries Weight Scale would be 1/8th of 31.10 grams (3.9 grams). A drachm on the Avoirdupois Weight Scale equates to 1/16th of 28.35 grams (1.8 grams). Thus C is correct.

Question 20

D

ADHD can be observed (see paragraph 2) – thus A is not correct. The statement in B is an interpretation of the last line in the second paragraph and is patently wrong. A smaller pre-frontal cortex does not mean a 'small brain' Moreover, not all children display all symptoms – hence the rest of the stamen is also incorrect. C is nullified by what is observed and also the science.

The information in the second last paragraph, taken with some of the other characteristics, listed in the text, indicates that D is indeed correct.

Question 21

B

A is meaningless as childhood is not an affliction for which there are 'symptoms'. The reference to amphetamines is as a Schedule 2 drug not in terms of harm caused, thus C is not correct. Whilst Ritalin may help some children to become less impulsive, so can dietary changes and behavioural modification. Thus, Ritalin is not required.

B is correct as it drives up dopamine levels in order to overcome the symptoms (as implied in paragraph 3).

Question 22

D

A cannot be I as the following two pieces of information (II and III) state that the ball goes higher and further with the same impetus. Hence D must be I as the flight should not be symmetrical. It would follow that C = II and B = III. This means that the answer is between C and D. Backspin, as shown by E, would give the ball lift and also make it move, upon hitting the ground it should bounce, with the spin, back towards the source. F indicates top-spin or overspin, hence D is correct.

Question 23

C

The future cannot be predicted from this text thus A must be discounted, as well as B (as it assumes the clothing will actually become a reality). D cannot be concluded from the text – rather, the scientists thought that they would start with heating people rather than buildings as an innovative approach. It is not clear whether such an approach is more effective or not.

It should be clear, and it is the premise of the research, that heating and energy consumption is a significant concern for scientists and thus C is correct.

Question 24

B

The main concern with respect to development (as opposed to design) is that benefits outweigh costs. Hence B should be correct from the application of common knowledge. A is hard to justify as what does 'high' mean – it is a relative concept. Why the development would be based on half the world's energy costs is a mystery – total cost is more important – hence C can be discounted. Whilst the US is a significant energy user and hence polluter, the issue of development does not vest with what the US opts to do or not do – hence D must also be discounted.

Question 25

D

Coughing cannot prevent emphysema (though it can prevent pneumonia) thus A must be discounted. The article is about encouraging coughing, but managing the inevitable pain, hence B must be discounted. There is nothing in the text to suggest that sneezing should be encouraged – rather it should be managed – hence C must be incorrect. D however is borne out by the text and is therefore correct. Coughing can clear the lungs but also places pressure on the sutures (stitches). Coughing can even open the stitches, so placing pressure on the wound will help to keep it from opening.

Question 26

B

Whilst hugging a pillow can help with managing pain through compression on the chest, pillows of themselves do not assist in recovery hence A is incorrect. There is nothing to suggest that bracing oneself will relive pressure on stitches hence C must be discounted as incorrect. Abdominal surgery has not relationship with sneezing or coughing thus D must be removed from consideration.

Holding the breath would be difficult after chest surgery as it would be painful. It is however encouraged, as is the slow release of breath.

Question 27

C

Curing lights can be used to activate peroxide and thus whiten teeth. However, most treatments do not use curing lights, thus A is incorrect. Whilst there are some side effects listed, there is no evidence that colour change must lead to side effects. Hence B cannot be correct. Whilst thermal sensitivity can be associated with the use of bleaching agents it is not a necessary fact and may or may not occur – hence D cannot be correct.

Paragraph four makes reference to successful at-home bleaching providing the regime is closely followed. Hence C is correct.

Question 28

B

High concentrations are stated to be in the order of 25%-40% hydrogen peroxide, whilst low hydrogen peroxide concentration is stated to be in the order of 3-6% and 3.5-6.5%. Given these figures, 38% is high concentration, eliminating D. 7% is too low to confidently fall in the medium concentration range, and 24% is too high. This eliminates A and C. Thus, the only confident estimation must be in the order of 10-20% - hence B or 18% must be correct.

Question 29

C

Taking the answers in order. If A was correct then it would mean that the brunette woman is telling the truth and that she loves travelling north. This must make the black haired woman's statement a lie. Since she stated that she loves travelling south, then if she is lying it must mean she actually loves travelling north. However, the facts as presented are that only one of the women loves travelling north. Hence A must be incorrect.

As regards B: If the black haired woman cannot be lying then she must be telling the truth. If this was the case then she must love travelling south. The brunette woman must be lying since at least one of the women is lying. Hence her statement that she loves travelling north must be a lie – she must actually love travelling south. However, this cannot be the case, as one of the women loves travelling north.

Taking D: if the brunette woman loves travelling south, then she is telling the truth. This is the same scenario as in B and so must be incorrect.

C must be correct: If both women are lying then the brunette woman actually loves travelling south (not north as she states) and the black haired woman must love travelling north (not south as she states). This also satisfies the condition that 'at least one of the women is lying'. Thus C is correct.

Question 30

D

A PDI of 16% for protein equates to 4 serves, as 1 serve equates to 4% of the percentage daily intake (PDI). Each serve is 4 squares. Thus 16% equates to 16 squares (4 x 4). Hence D is corrects.

Question 31

B

The Calorie equivalence of the average adult is 8,700kJ. In the last right-hand column there is information that 100g of the product equates to 2,240kJ or just over one quarter of the PDI as measured in kilojoules (kJ). Hence 400g of the product would be required.

We are told that the serving size is 25g and that there are 8.8 serves per package. This equates to 220 grams. Hence, 2 packages would be 440 grams. Just over 1.9 packages would be required to give the energy equivalence. Hence B is correct.

Question 32

A

There is nothing in the data that suggests world records will meet the project times either faster or slower than predicted or even if they will ever be achieved. Hence D must be eliminated. Given the data set, with predictions for 2000, 2028 and 2040, and the current world records the following should be clear: for all distances except 800m, 1000m and 10,000m the current records fall between the predictions in 2000 and 2028. Thus C can be eliminated. A close look at the times for the shortest distances (100m are 200m) closer to the 2028 projections than 2000 and thus are significantly ahead of project times. A close look at the times on the longest distances (21,100m and 42,195m) shows that, whilst the times fall between 2000 and 2028 projections – they are closer to the middle (assuming linearity) and hence are not significantly lower than projected times.

Hence A must be correct.

Question 33

B

Nothing can be said with any certainty about whether or if records will be broken in the future – hence A must be eliminated. There is no evidence on training regimes or dietary effects and thus C cannot be correct. As with A, no predication can be made on whether a record will be broken, thus D must be incorrect.

A close look at when world records have been created reveals that all except two have been set in August or September – the second half of the year. This must mean that specific events (world championships, Olympic games and so forth) must be on in that time of the year. Hence B is correct.

Question 34

B

The numbers are compiled as follows: 521525: this is 5^1 (5), 5^2 (25) and 5^3 (125) consecutively and the digits _**reversed**_. The same holds for the next number: 46614 – which is 4^1 (4), 4^2 (16) and 4^3 (64) consecutively with the digits reversed. The third number, 8293 is 3^1 (3), 3^2 (9) and 3^3 (27) all reversed. Similarly, 842 is 2^1 (2), 2^2 (2) and 2^3 (8) in reverse. Thus, the answer should be 1^1 (1), 1^2 (1) and 1^3 (1) consecutively and reversed - or simply 111 as shown in B.

Question 35

A

II and V are not relevant hence B and D can be eliminated. Since statement III is true, statement VII is irrelevant and hence eliminates C. So, why is A correct? Taking the statements from the introductory text and using the additional information reveals: Lago is bigger than Ohno but smaller than Uboo. Nogo is the largest town (III) and there is one town larger than Uboo. This means in order the two largest towns must be Nago followed by Uboo. Now, if there is one town smaller than Jolo then it must be Ohno as Lago is bigger than Ohno and must also be bigger than Jolo if Jolo is the second smallest town. This means that in size from largest to smallest the order is:

Nogo, Uboo, Lago, Jolo and Ohno – hence Lago is bigger than Jolo and smaller than Nogo. To work this out all that is required is statement I, III, IV and VI – hence A is correct.

Question 36

D

Whilst aluminium is absorbed and can cause estrogen-like effects, it cannot be conclusively concluded (though it has been suggested by some scientists) that this causes the growth of cancer cells. Hence A must be discounted, as it is incorrect. Antiperspirants block the sweat ducts rather than killing bacteria, hence B is also incorrect. There is nothing in the text referring to the compounds made by aluminium and parabens thus C cannot be concluded. As regards D: parabens have been shown to mimic the effects of estrogen in the body's cells. Thus, butylparaben – a paraben – will copy (mimic) the effects of estrogen in body cells (regardless of the gender).

Question 37

A

There is no need for researchers to develop aluminium-free products unless it can be proven that there is a conclusive link between aluminium and breast cancer. Thus B and C can be eliminated from consideration. Whilst estrogen has the ability to promote the growth of cancer cells, there is nothing to suggest that estrogen *per se* is the issue – hence D is not correct. If it can be proven that aluminium causes breast cancer then informed decisions can be made – thus A is correct.

Question 38

C

The trick here is to add the numbers to get 200 and then multiply. Thus, 199 + 1 = 200. Similarly, 198 + 2 = 200, 197 + 3 = 200, 196 + 4 = 200, etc. This would be the case all the way to 99 + 101.

There are therefore 99 lots of 200. However, there is also the actual number 200, hence there are 100 lots of 200 in total. This adds to 20,000. The only other numbers to add to this are 100 (which has not yet been added) and 201. Hence the answer is 20,301 or C.

Question 39

C

There is no stead or predictable trend to the graph showing the size of household debt in the period December 1987 to December 2013, hence A can be eliminated. No reliable conclusions can be made in regards to average household debt thus B must be incorrect. There is no evidence provided about the GFC (which occurred in the period 2009 to 2011) and its effect on falls in household debt, hence D must be eliminated.

Looking at the first graph, the steepest growth in household debt (evidenced by the highest gradient of the line) occurred between December 2007 and December 2009, hence C must hold true and is therefore correct.

Question 40

C

There is no data about the relationship between the value of household income and household assets hence A must be incorrect. There is no evidence on what has happened to the value of household income, thus B cannot be correct. Furthermore, there can be no general statement made about how risk averse or not people have become (it could be the case, for example, that lenders are lending less). As regards C: In December 2013the size of household debt compared to annual income was near enough to 180%. If debt was frozen and all income was applied to pay it off then it would take 1.8 years or one year and 10 months – hence C is correct.

Question 41

C

The first diagram indicates that ischaemic heart disease is responsible for about 15% of ALL deaths (not just those from heart disease) hence A and B can be eliminated. The second diagram indicated that ischaemic heart disease (IHD) is responsible for a high proportion of deaths that result from heart disease (about 85%) thus D is incorrect and C is correct.

Question 42

D

Whilst the research indicates that antibiotic resistance is rising, there is no suggestion that its use should be stopped altogether – hence A can be eliminated. As regards B: there has already been close monitoring of the use and effects of antibiotics as WHO has undertaken comprehensive studies – hence B can be eliminated. There is no statement made to the effect that antibiotics cannot be used to effectively treat pneumonia, thus C can be eliminated. It should be clear from the text that antibiotics are of decreased effectiveness over time - hence D is correct.

Question 43

A

The textual reference is that "in some parts of the country (Australia) 80 per cent of staph infections cannot be treated with standard antibiotics" – this eliminates B which is too generalised a statement. There is no evidence that bloodstream infections are on the increase – thus C is not correct. Whilst urinary tract infections are harder to treat, there is no evidence that they cannot be treated – thus D is also not correct.

As regards A: superbugs come from bacteria becoming resistant to antibiotics in all nations where they are used extensively – including Australia. Moreover, when people return to Australia from holidays they can bring 'superbugs' into Australia – hence A is correct.

Question 44

C

As nanobots have not actually been developed then A can be discounted, as can B as well as D. Only C captures the thrust of the article – the nanobots are being designed – but have not been developed.

Question 45

D

There is nothing in the text to effectively conclude that doctors won't be required. If that was the case then doctors would hardly be 'fizzing with excitement' – hence A can be eliminated. B and C are far too certain to be reasonably concluded thus they can be removed from consideration. There is every likelihood that should they be developed then there will be a version that is designed to specifically distinguish cancer cells from normal cells in order to effectively destroy them – thus D is correct.

Question 46

A

There is nothing to suggest that nanorobots must be of any particular size to be successful in the medical field thus B is incorrect. There is also no comparison of which nanobots doing what would be most effective thus C must be eliminated. No reference is made to the elimination of toothpaste hence D is not right at all.

There are reference to non-medical uses of nanotechnologies thus A is clearly correct.

Question 47

B

Whilst the likelihood of death can be high – there is no certainty a person will die if contracting Ebola – hence A is not correct. Since not all chimpanzees, gorillas, fruit bats or monkey are Ebola infected then it does not follow that people should not touch them – hence C is not correct. There can be several reasons as to why blood might ooze from gums (overuse of an electric toothbrush, use of dental floss, hitting oneself in the mouth with a high-speed, plastic-coated marshmallow☺, and so on) hence D cannot be the diagnosis for Ebola. This should also be clear from the six investigations at the bottom of the factsheet. Thus D can be eliminated.

As regards B: since the incubation period can be from 2 to 21 days then a person can be infected and show no sighs for 21 days. This would mean that on the 22nd day they would have symptoms and thus be infectious – hence B is correct.

Question 48

D

Since all fruit bats do not have Ebola then A cannot be correct. Health care workers must take appropriate precautions – but it does not follow that they are at high risk hence B is not correct. Again, with C, laboratory technicians should only take great precautions when dealing with samples from Ebola infected patients – not all samples from all patients – hence C cannot be correct either. The text does make reference to people at burial ceremonies making direct contact with the body of a person who died as a result of Ebola – thus D is correct.

Essential Preparation for

UMAT

UNDERGRADUATE MEDICINE & HEALTH SCIENCES ADMISSION TEST

MULTIPLE CHOICE ANSWER SHEET

Use pencil when filling out this sheet

Fill in the circle correctly
● Ⓑ Ⓒ Ⓓ

If you make a mistake neatly cross it out and circle the correct response
✖ ● Ⓒ Ⓓ

1 Ⓐ Ⓑ Ⓒ Ⓓ   25 Ⓐ Ⓑ Ⓒ Ⓓ
2 Ⓐ Ⓑ Ⓒ Ⓓ   26 Ⓐ Ⓑ Ⓒ Ⓓ
3 Ⓐ Ⓑ Ⓒ Ⓓ   27 Ⓐ Ⓑ Ⓒ Ⓓ
4 Ⓐ Ⓑ Ⓒ Ⓓ   28 Ⓐ Ⓑ Ⓒ Ⓓ
5 Ⓐ Ⓑ Ⓒ Ⓓ   29 Ⓐ Ⓑ Ⓒ Ⓓ
6 Ⓐ Ⓑ Ⓒ Ⓓ   30 Ⓐ Ⓑ Ⓒ Ⓓ
7 Ⓐ Ⓑ Ⓒ Ⓓ   31 Ⓐ Ⓑ Ⓒ Ⓓ
8 Ⓐ Ⓑ Ⓒ Ⓓ   32 Ⓐ Ⓑ Ⓒ Ⓓ
9 Ⓐ Ⓑ Ⓒ Ⓓ   33 Ⓐ Ⓑ Ⓒ Ⓓ
10 Ⓐ Ⓑ Ⓒ Ⓓ   34 Ⓐ Ⓑ Ⓒ Ⓓ
11 Ⓐ Ⓑ Ⓒ Ⓓ   35 Ⓐ Ⓑ Ⓒ Ⓓ
12 Ⓐ Ⓑ Ⓒ Ⓓ   36 Ⓐ Ⓑ Ⓒ Ⓓ
13 Ⓐ Ⓑ Ⓒ Ⓓ   37 Ⓐ Ⓑ Ⓒ Ⓓ
14 Ⓐ Ⓑ Ⓒ Ⓓ   38 Ⓐ Ⓑ Ⓒ Ⓓ
15 Ⓐ Ⓑ Ⓒ Ⓓ   39 Ⓐ Ⓑ Ⓒ Ⓓ
16 Ⓐ Ⓑ Ⓒ Ⓓ   40 Ⓐ Ⓑ Ⓒ Ⓓ
17 Ⓐ Ⓑ Ⓒ Ⓓ   41 Ⓐ Ⓑ Ⓒ Ⓓ
18 Ⓐ Ⓑ Ⓒ Ⓓ   42 Ⓐ Ⓑ Ⓒ Ⓓ
19 Ⓐ Ⓑ Ⓒ Ⓓ   43 Ⓐ Ⓑ Ⓒ Ⓓ
20 Ⓐ Ⓑ Ⓒ Ⓓ   44 Ⓐ Ⓑ Ⓒ Ⓓ
21 Ⓐ Ⓑ Ⓒ Ⓓ   45 Ⓐ Ⓑ Ⓒ Ⓓ
22 Ⓐ Ⓑ Ⓒ Ⓓ   46 Ⓐ Ⓑ Ⓒ Ⓓ
23 Ⓐ Ⓑ Ⓒ Ⓓ   47 Ⓐ Ⓑ Ⓒ Ⓓ
24 Ⓐ Ⓑ Ⓒ Ⓓ   48 Ⓐ Ⓑ Ⓒ Ⓓ

Essential Preparation for

UMAT

UNDERGRADUATE MEDICINE & HEALTH SCIENCES ADMISSION TEST

MULTIPLE CHOICE ANSWER SHEET

1 (A) (B) (C) (D)
2 (A) (B) (C) (D)
3 (A) (B) (C) (D)
4 (A) (B) (C) (D)
5 (A) (B) (C) (D)
6 (A) (B) (C) (D)
7 (A) (B) (C) (D)
8 (A) (B) (C) (D)
9 (A) (B) (C) (D)
10 (A) (B) (C) (D)
11 (A) (B) (C) (D)
12 (A) (B) (C) (D)
13 (A) (B) (C) (D)
14 (A) (B) (C) (D)
15 (A) (B) (C) (D)
16 (A) (B) (C) (D)
17 (A) (B) (C) (D)
18 (A) (B) (C) (D)
19 (A) (B) (C) (D)
20 (A) (B) (C) (D)
21 (A) (B) (C) (D)
22 (A) (B) (C) (D)
23 (A) (B) (C) (D)
24 (A) (B) (C) (D)

25 (A) (B) (C) (D)
26 (A) (B) (C) (D)
27 (A) (B) (C) (D)
28 (A) (B) (C) (D)
29 (A) (B) (C) (D)
30 (A) (B) (C) (D)
31 (A) (B) (C) (D)
32 (A) (B) (C) (D)
33 (A) (B) (C) (D)
34 (A) (B) (C) (D)
35 (A) (B) (C) (D)
36 (A) (B) (C) (D)
37 (A) (B) (C) (D)
38 (A) (B) (C) (D)
39 (A) (B) (C) (D)
40 (A) (B) (C) (D)
41 (A) (B) (C) (D)
42 (A) (B) (C) (D)
43 (A) (B) (C) (D)
44 (A) (B) (C) (D)
45 (A) (B) (C) (D)
46 (A) (B) (C) (D)
47 (A) (B) (C) (D)
48 (A) (B) (C) (D)

UMAT

UNDERGRADUATE MEDICINE & HEALTH SCIENCES ADMISSION TEST

MULTIPLE CHOICE ANSWER SHEET

Use pencil when filling out this sheet

Fill in the circle correctly
● Ⓑ Ⓒ Ⓓ

If you make a mistake neatly cross it out and circle the correct response
⊗ ● Ⓒ Ⓓ

1	Ⓐ Ⓑ Ⓒ Ⓓ			25	Ⓐ Ⓑ Ⓒ Ⓓ
2	Ⓐ Ⓑ Ⓒ Ⓓ			26	Ⓐ Ⓑ Ⓒ Ⓓ
3	Ⓐ Ⓑ Ⓒ Ⓓ			27	Ⓐ Ⓑ Ⓒ Ⓓ
4	Ⓐ Ⓑ Ⓒ Ⓓ			28	Ⓐ Ⓑ Ⓒ Ⓓ
5	Ⓐ Ⓑ Ⓒ Ⓓ			29	Ⓐ Ⓑ Ⓒ Ⓓ
6	Ⓐ Ⓑ Ⓒ Ⓓ			30	Ⓐ Ⓑ Ⓒ Ⓓ
7	Ⓐ Ⓑ Ⓒ Ⓓ			31	Ⓐ Ⓑ Ⓒ Ⓓ
8	Ⓐ Ⓑ Ⓒ Ⓓ			32	Ⓐ Ⓑ Ⓒ Ⓓ
9	Ⓐ Ⓑ Ⓒ Ⓓ			33	Ⓐ Ⓑ Ⓒ Ⓓ
10	Ⓐ Ⓑ Ⓒ Ⓓ			34	Ⓐ Ⓑ Ⓒ Ⓓ
11	Ⓐ Ⓑ Ⓒ Ⓓ			35	Ⓐ Ⓑ Ⓒ Ⓓ
12	Ⓐ Ⓑ Ⓒ Ⓓ			36	Ⓐ Ⓑ Ⓒ Ⓓ
13	Ⓐ Ⓑ Ⓒ Ⓓ			37	Ⓐ Ⓑ Ⓒ Ⓓ
14	Ⓐ Ⓑ Ⓒ Ⓓ			38	Ⓐ Ⓑ Ⓒ Ⓓ
15	Ⓐ Ⓑ Ⓒ Ⓓ			39	Ⓐ Ⓑ Ⓒ Ⓓ
16	Ⓐ Ⓑ Ⓒ Ⓓ			40	Ⓐ Ⓑ Ⓒ Ⓓ
17	Ⓐ Ⓑ Ⓒ Ⓓ			41	Ⓐ Ⓑ Ⓒ Ⓓ
18	Ⓐ Ⓑ Ⓒ Ⓓ			42	Ⓐ Ⓑ Ⓒ Ⓓ
19	Ⓐ Ⓑ Ⓒ Ⓓ			43	Ⓐ Ⓑ Ⓒ Ⓓ
20	Ⓐ Ⓑ Ⓒ Ⓓ			44	Ⓐ Ⓑ Ⓒ Ⓓ
21	Ⓐ Ⓑ Ⓒ Ⓓ			45	Ⓐ Ⓑ Ⓒ Ⓓ
22	Ⓐ Ⓑ Ⓒ Ⓓ			46	Ⓐ Ⓑ Ⓒ Ⓓ
23	Ⓐ Ⓑ Ⓒ Ⓓ			47	Ⓐ Ⓑ Ⓒ Ⓓ
24	Ⓐ Ⓑ Ⓒ Ⓓ			48	Ⓐ Ⓑ Ⓒ Ⓓ